Curl-Up quilts

Flannel Appliqué & More from Piece O' Cake Designs

Becky Goldsmith & Linda Jenkins

C&T PUBLISHING

Text and Artwork © 2004 Becky Goldsmith and Linda Jenkins

Artwork © 2004 C&T Publishing, Inc.

Publisher: Amy Marson

Editorial Director: Gailen Runge

Editor: Lynn Koolish

Technical Editors: Sara Kate MacFarland, Carolyn Aune

Copyeditor/Proofreader: Stacy Chamness/Wordfirm

Cover Designer: Kristen Yenche

Design Director: Dave Nash

Production Artist: Kirstie L. McCormick

Illustrators: Becky Goldsmith and Tim Manibusan

Production Assistant: Luke Mulks

Quilt Photography: Sharon Risedorph unless otherwise noted

How-to Photography: Luke Mulks and Kirstie McCormick

Published by C&T Publishing, Inc., P.O. Box 1456, Lafayette, California 94549

Front cover: *Sunny Days* quilt by Linda Jenkins, pillows by Becky Goldsmith,
    photo by Diane Pedersen

Back cover: *Wonderful Wooly Pincushions* by Becky Goldsmith, photos by Kirstie L. McCormick;
    Meow & Woof by Linda Jenkins; *Sweet Pea* by Becky Goldsmith

Library of Congress Cataloging-in-Publication Data

Goldsmith, Becky.
  Curl-up quilts : flannel appliqué & more from Piece O' Cake Designs /
Becky Goldsmith and Linda Jenkins.
      p. cm.
  Includes bibliographical references and index.
  ISBN 1-57120-264-1 (paper trade)
  1. Appliqué--Patterns. 2. Quilting. 3. Flannel. I. Title: Flannel
appliqué and more from Piece O' Cake Designs. II. Jenkins, Linda. III. Piece
O'Cake Designs. IV. Title.

TT779.G62958 2004
746.46'041--dc22

2004004522

Printed in China   10 9 8 7 6 5 4 3 2 1

Table of Contents

Acknowledgments

A great big thank you to Lynn Koolish, our editor at C&T. Lynn suggested that we write this book. With Lynn's suggestion we discovered how much fun it is to work with flannel!

Our technical editor, Sara Kate MacFarland, made sure that we got the details right. It would be nice to be perfect, but we aren't, so we are grateful to have Sara double-checking us. Kirstie McCormick, this book's designer, has given Curl-Up Quilts its distinctive appearance. We love the cover that Kris Yenche designed. Luke Mulks, the production assistant, kept all the many ducks in a row to make the publication of this book go smoothly. We thank you all for your excellent efforts.

We thank Irwin Bear at P&B Textiles for sharing his knowledge about how flannel is made. Thanks to the folks at P&B, Robert Kaufman Co., and Moda for being so helpful and generous with their flannel; we couldn't have made these quilts without the fabric. Also, the helpful folks at the Warm & Natural Company and H.D. Wilbanks at Hobbs Bonded Fibers deserve a big thank you for providing us with wonderful cotton batting.

Introduction

Flannel is cozy and casual. It brings to mind winter nights and being curled up in your favorite chair by a warm fire, stitching in hand—wearing cute flannel pajamas of course!

Quilts and flannel go together. Both are soft and warm—and flannel is extra-cuddly. Flannel cries out to be touched and snuggled under. Quilts made from flannel are quilts that are going to be used and loved. They make great gifts. In fact, we made the quilts in this book for special people in our lives.

Flannel is great in pieced quilts, and you are going to be surprised at just how wonderful it is to appliqué. Working with flannel is a little bit different from working with other cotton fabric, so be sure to read about working with flannel on pages 7–9.

Have you seen the beautiful wool fabric in quilt shops? We couldn't help but notice the wonderful rich colors and the great texture of these wools. Flannel and wool look so good together we just had to include some wool in this book.

So now is the time to sit down, get comfortable, and start planning your curl-up quilts!

Basic Supplies

Fabric: All of the fabrics used in these quilts are 100% cotton flannel unless otherwise noted.

Wool: We found two kinds of machine-washable wool. One is made from wool fabric that is woven (like men's suit fabric) and then felted. The other is made from wool fibers that are felted together—there is no obvious woven base. The woven wool is much easier to machine piece.

Appliqué thread: Use cotton thread with cotton fabric. There are many brands to choose from. Work with different brands until you find the one that works best for you. For hand appliqué, we like both Mettler 60-weight machine embroidery thread and DMC 50-weight machine embroidery thread.

Machine quilting thread: Use cotton thread with cotton fabric. We used a variety of threads in our flannel quilts. In general we found that a slightly thicker thread looked best on the flannel.

Batting: Flannel is thicker and heavier than regular cotton fabric is. A thin batt works best. We noted our choices in the project chapters. Quilt a sample block before basting the quilt.

Needles: For hand appliqué, we use a size 11 Hemming & Son milliners needle. There are many good needles. Find the one that fits **your** hand.

Pins: Use ½" sequin pins to pin the appliqué pieces in place. Use larger flower-head quilting pins to hold the positioning overlay in place.

Fusible web: If you prefer to fuse and machine stitch the appliqué, use a paper-backed fusible web. Choose the one you like best and follow the directions on the package. It's a good idea to test the fusible web on the flannel you will be using.

Non-stick pressing sheet: If you are doing fusible appliqué, a non-stick pressing sheet will protect the iron and ironing board.

Scissors: Use embroidery-size scissors for both paper and fabric. Small, sharp scissors are better for intricate cutting.

Rotary cutter, mat, and acrylic ruler: When trimming blocks to size and cutting borders, rotary cutting tools will give you the best results.

Pencils: We use either a General's Charcoal White pencil, a Stabilo Aquarellable white pencil, or an Ultimate Mechanical Pencil for Quilters to draw around templates onto the fabric.

Permanent markers: To make the positioning overlay, a Sharpie Ultra Fine Point Permanent Marker works best on the upholstery vinyl.

Permanent black gel pen: To draw the pupils in the eyes of the dogs and cats in *Meow & Woof*.

Clear upholstery vinyl: Use 54"-wide, clear, medium-weight upholstery vinyl to make the positioning overlay. You can usually find it in stores that carry upholstery fabric.

Clear heavyweight self-laminating sheets: Use these sheets to make templates. You can find them at most office supply stores and sometimes at warehouse markets. Buy the single-sided sheets, not the pouches. If you can't find the laminate, use clear Contac paper.

Sandpaper board: When tracing templates onto fabric, place the fabric on the sandpaper side of the board. Then place the template on the fabric. You'll love the way the sandpaper holds the fabric in place when you trace.

Wooden toothpick: Use a round toothpick to help turn under the turn-under allowance at points and curves. Wood has a texture that grabs and holds.

Full-spectrum work light: These lamps give off a bright and natural light. A floor lamp is particularly nice as you can position it over your shoulder. Appliqué is so much easier when you can see what you are doing.

Cotton quilting gloves: These gloves make it easier to hold onto the quilt during machine quilting.

Appliqué supplies

About Flannel

What Makes Flannel Different?

All fabric has a thread count, how many threads there are per square inch. Thread count varies from company to company and from fabric to fabric. Greige (pronounced gray) goods is the term for the base cloth a design is printed on.

Greige goods for regular cotton quilt fabric commonly have 68 x 68 threads per square inch using a 1-ply yarn. A heavier cloth is often 60 x 60 threads per inch made from a slightly heavier 1-ply yarn. The higher numbers indicate a tighter, finer fabric. The more threads per square inch, the better the coverage.

Flannel is usually 42 x 43 threads per square inch. Heavier flannels can be 42 x 46 using a heavier 2-ply yarn. Some flannels use a single/double yarn, meaning that the yarn is single-ply in one direction and double-ply in the other. You might think that single/double fabric would be thinner; however, the fabric is back-filled with resins for fullness.

Flannel fabric is "napped" with brushes that break up the surface fibers. This gives flannel its distinctive fuzzy appearance. The fabric is printed, then napped again on one or both sides. It can be double-napped and/or single-napped. These decisions are based on what the finished fabric is supposed to look like.

So What?

What it boils down to is that flannel has a low thread count so it can have a nap. A finer fabric with a higher thread count cannot have the same cozy nap that flannel does. Because of the lower thread count, flannel is thick, a little bit stretchy, and it ravels easily. However, this isn't all bad.

The heavier threads in the fabric combined with the nap make the appliqué stitches invisible. You will be amazed! The appliqué stitches will be a little longer than usual because the fabric is heavier—so the appliqué will be a little faster. It is true that the outer points will be a bit rounder, but that's okay. Flannel is a casual fabric that doesn't necessarily lend itself to crispness.

Flannel ravels. That is its nature. For that reason we prefer to turn under the edges of our appliqué. The appliqué is more stable, and we don't have little bits of thread all over us—and the furniture.

To fight flannel's tendency to stretch, treat the fabric gently. Be careful not to pull it out of shape as you work with it. On the plus side, the stretchiness makes it easier to ease in extra fullness when you have to. Once the top is together, be careful how you handle it. Don't hold it up by one edge, allowing the weight of the top to stretch it out of shape.

Color and Flannel

The variety of flannel fabric is growing, but it is true there are not as many color choices in flannel as there are in regular cotton fabrics. We took this as a challenge. Working within a limited color palette is in some ways easier. Having fewer color choices forces you to be creative with the choices available.

But what if you *really need* a color that just isn't available in flannel? We decided that it was okay to "cheat" just a little bit. Linda used a few woven, but not flannel, plaids and stripes in *Fruit Trees* because she needed the colors in them. Be careful when mixing the lighter fabrics with the heavier flannels. It could cause the quilt to be wavy. But when it comes to color, a quilter's got to do what a quilter's got to do!

To Fuse or Not To Fuse

Flannel's softness makes it special. Fused appliqué is almost always stiffer to the touch, so you lose some of that softness. In addition, fused flannels do not always stick together well. If the nap on the fabric is heavy, the fusible web adheres to the nap but not the body of the fabric. For these reasons we have reservations about fusing flannel.

If you do choose to use fusible web with flannel, please test the fabrics you plan to use. We recommend that you stitch around the outside of all fused appliqué pieces either by hand or machine. A blanket stitch looks nice.

Fabric Preparation

Prewash the fabric before using it. Prewashing is not only a good way to test for colorfastness, but to check shrinkage rates. Flannel will shrink. Different flannels shrink at different rates. It's better if the fabric shrinks *before* it is sewn into the quilt. Prewashed fabric has a better hand, is easier to appliqué, and smells better. Yardages given for the projects in this book are generous enough to allow for normal shrinkage.

Flannel will ravel as it is washed. All those loose threads tangle together and can be a bother. Washing flannel in the gentle cycle can help. The fabric will be agitated less, which will help cut down on the frays and tangles. Linda chose not to agitate her fabric at all. Here's how: Fill the washer with water and soap, put the fabric in, and let it soak. Next turn the washer to spin. Rinse and repeat the soaking and spin. This way you never agitate the fabric.

All of the wool we bought was machine washable. We prewashed it the same way we would regular cotton fabric.

Both the flannel and the wool fabrics are very linty. Clean the lint trap in the dryer often as they are drying. And keep in mind that you may need to clean the bobbin area of the sewing machine more often than normal, too.

About Our Fabric Requirements

Cotton fabric is usually 40" to 44" wide off the bolt. Some flannels and wools are 56" wide. To be safe, we calculated all of our fabric requirements based on a 40" width.

Use the fabric requirements for each quilt as a guide, but remember that the yardage amounts will vary depending on how many fabrics you use and the sizes of the pieces you cut. Our measurements allow for both fabric shrinkage and a few errors in cutting.

Seam Allowances

All piecing is designed for ¼" seam allowances. However, flannel and wool are thicker than normal cotton fabric. Where pieced blocks are part of the quilt, make a sample block. Check the size of the sample to make sure that the blocks are going to be the correct size. Adjust the seam allowance as necessary. We found that by using a scant ¼" seam allowance, our blocks were more accurate.

Borders

The cutting instructions in this book are mathematically correct. However, variations in the finished size of the quilt top can result from slight differences in seam allowances, the amount of piecing, and the thickness of the fabric. Flannel in particular can stretch.

The measurements provided should be very close to your actual quilt size, but you should always measure *your* quilt before adding sashing and borders. If the borders are pieced (as many in this book are), you need to be sure that your pieced borders fit with the pieced quilt tops. The inner borders can be adjusted to account for piecing inconsistencies. If the borders are not pieced, you can measure your quilt, then cut sashings and/or borders to fit.

When measuring, be sure to measure the inside of the quilt top or block, not the outer edges that can more easily stretch. Read the cutting and assembly instructions carefully before cutting sashings and borders.

Pressing Flannel and Wool

Be gentle when pressing flannel and wool because they stretch. Be especially careful at the edges of blocks and border strips. **Instead of pressing the fabric "out" and stretching it, press "down."**

Should you use steam when you press? Maybe. We have each had different experiences with steam. It is very possible that the amount of humidity where you live, combined with the steam in the iron, will affect how steaming works for you. Some irons put out more steam than others. The padding on the ironing board (or lack thereof) can have an effect. There are too many variables for a hard-and-fast rule. The best advice we have is to make test samples using your own iron and fabric and find the best way to press so the fabric won't be stretched.

Quilting Flannel

You are going to love hearing this: **Flannel quilts look better with less, rather than more, quilting!** A flannel quilt with too much quilting loses its softness. Less quilting means you finish the quilt faster!

We tried a variety of batting materials in our quilts. With more unquilted areas in the quilt, you must choose an appropriate batting. Flannel is a heavier fabric, so a lighter batting is often called for. After some trial and error we found that we liked the Warm & Natural Cotton the best.

We listed the specific batting we used in the materials section for each quilt, but we strongly suggest that you quilt a sample block using your primary background fabric, your backing fabric, and the batting of your choice. Those of you in colder climates may want a warmer quilt than those of you down South would.

Wool Log Cabin

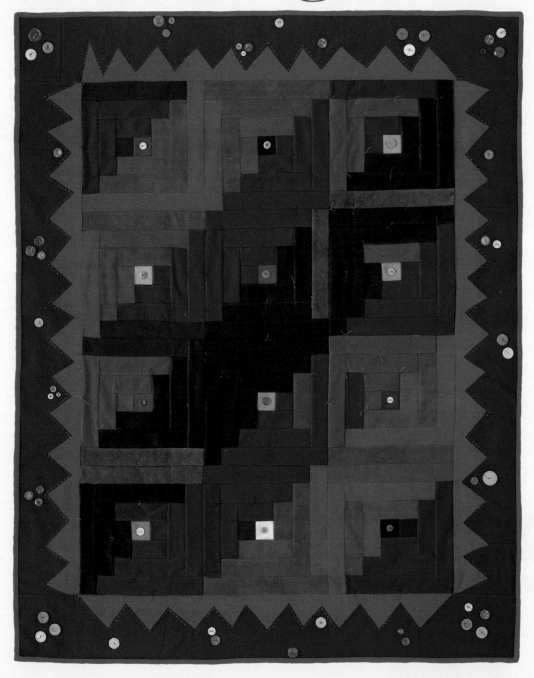

Made by Linda Jenkins, 2003

Finished block size: 12¼" x 12¼"

Finished quilt size: 49¾" x 62"

Wool comes in such a luscious range of colors and feels so good in your hands! Who can resist it? The simplicity of this Log Cabin block is the perfect showcase for these great pieces of wool.

Materials

Wool:

    Center squares: light green, teal, gold, orange, yellow, and light purple scraps

    Blue logs and border background: 2⅜ yards

    Navy logs: ⅓ yard

    Light blue center square and logs: ⅓ yard

    Green center square and logs: ⅝ yard

    Olive logs: ⅓ yard

    Reds for logs: 1 yard total (Linda used at least 2 in her quilt)

    Pink logs: ⅛ yard

    Dark purple logs: ¼ yard

Red flannel:

    Zigzag inner border: 1¾ yards

    Backing: 4 yards

    Binding: 1 yard

Perle cotton in size 8 or 10 to tie the quilt

Buttons in various sizes and colors: approximately 65

What kind of wool should I buy?

We found two kinds of machine-washable wool in the quilt shops we visited. One kind of wool is made from wool fabric that is woven (like men's suit fabric) and then felted. It is soft and drapes well. The second kind of wool is made from wool fibers that are felted together—there is no obvious woven base. This kind of wool is stiffer. The woven wool is much easier to machine piece.

Cutting

Log Cabin Blocks

Each block is made up of 13 units. The color combinations in each block are different.

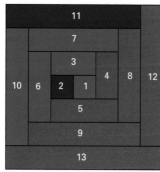

Each block is made up of 13 units.

Unit 1: 2¼" x 2¼" square
Cut 1 from each of the following colors: light green, teal, orange, yellow, light blue, and light purple.
Cut 2 from each of the following colors: green, gold, and red.

Unit 2: 2¼" x 2¼" square
Cut 3 navy squares.
Cut 8 blue squares.
Cut 1 light blue square.

Unit 3: 2¼" x 4" strips
Cut 11 blue strips.
Cut 1 light blue strip.

Unit 4: 2¼" x 4" strips
Cut 6 red strips.
Cut 6 green strips.

Unit 5: 2¼" x 5¾" strips
Cut 7 red strips.
Cut 1 dark purple strip.
Cut 4 green strips.

Unit 6: 2¼" x 5¾" strips
Cut 8 blue strips.
Cut 2 light blue strips.
Cut 1 navy strip.
Cut 1 red strip.

Unit 7: 2¼" x 7½" strips
Cut 10 blue strips.
Cut 2 light blue strips.

Unit 8: 2¼" x 7½" strips
Cut 6 red strips.
Cut 6 green strips.

Unit 9: 2¼" x 9¼" strips
Cut 6 red strips.
Cut 6 green strips.
Cut 1 light blue strip.

Unit 10: 2¼" x 9¼" strips
Cut 9 blue strips.
Cut 2 light blue strips.
Cut 1 dark purple strip.

Unit 11: 2¼" x 11" strips
Cut 3 navy strips.
Cut 9 blue strips.

Unit 12: 2¼" x 11" strips
Cut 6 red strips.
Cut 5 green strips.
Cut 1 olive strip.

Unit 13: 2¼" x 12¾" strips
Cut 5 red strips.
Cut 1 pink strip.
Cut 3 olive strips.
Cut 3 green strips.

Red flannel zigzag inner border
*Measure your quilt top before
cutting these borders.*
Cut 2 side border strips lengthwise
4¼" x 49½".
Cut 2 top/bottom border strips
lengthwise 4¼" x about 37¼".

Blue outer border fabric
Cut 2 side border strips lengthwise
8" x 51".
Cut 2 top/bottom border strips
lengthwise 8" x 54¾".

Binding fabric
Cut 1 square 31" x 31" to make
3"-wide continuous-bias binding
240" long. (Refer to pages 71–72
for instructions.)

Block and Border Assembly
Log Cabin Blocks
Press the seam allowances away
from the center of the block. If
pressing with steam stretches the
wool, press with a dry iron.

Work around the block in a clock-
wise direction. The blocks are
numbered from left to right, from
top to bottom. Arrange the different colored strips for each block as
shown in the illustration below.

1. Sew unit 1 to unit 2. Press.

2. Sew unit 3 to the block. Press.

3. Continue in this manner until all
of the logs have been sewn to the
block.

4. Refer to the Quilt Assembly
Diagram and sew blocks together
into rows. Press.

5. Sew rows together. Press.

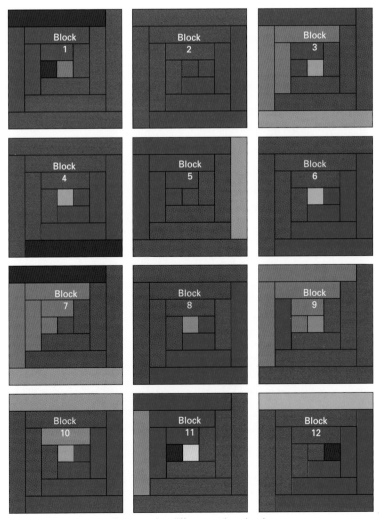

*Arrange the different colored strips
for each block as shown.*

Zigzag Inner Border

Refer to Borders on page 8 for instructions on measuring your quilt top and cutting borders to size as needed.

1. The zigzag inner border is designed so the finished ends match the finished edges of the inside of the quilt. Measure the quilt. Cut the red zigzag strips lengthwise 4½" x the height and width of the quilt, including a ³⁄₁₆" turn-under allowance at each end of all strips.

2. Press each outer border strip in half to find the center.

3. Press each red flannel zigzag strip in half to find the center.

4. Draw a random zigzag design on one long side of each red flannel strip. Leave room for a ³⁄₁₆" turn-under allowance. Do not trim away any excess fabric.

Draw a random zigzag on one long side of each red flannel strip.

5. Match the centers of a side outer border with a side zigzag strip.

Match the centers of the borders.

6. Pin the strip in place, then baste the strip. Remove the pins.

Baste the zigzag strip in place.

7. Use the cutaway appliqué technique shown on page 69 to appliqué the edge of the zigzag. Repeat for each border.

Quilt Assembly

Refer to the Quilt Assembly Diagram for quilt construction.

1. Sew a side border strip to each side of the quilt. Be sure to center the zigzag inner border; the excess will be trimmed after all the borders are sewn. Press the seam allowances toward the outer border.

2. Sew on the top and bottom borders. Be sure to center the zigzag inner border. Press toward the inner border.

3. Trim all outer borders to 6½" wide.

4. Baste the layers of the quilt together. (Refer to page 68 for instructions.) Tie the quilt with perle cotton as necessary to hold the layers together. Linda used a long running stitch in matching perle cotton on the border just outside of the red zigzag.

5. Attach the binding with a ³⁄₈" seam allowance because of the thickness of the wool.

6. Sleeves don't work particularly well on tied quilts unless there are many ties spaced closely together. Consider adding tabs to the top edge of the back of the quilt if you intend to hang it.

7. Tie buttons to the quilt.

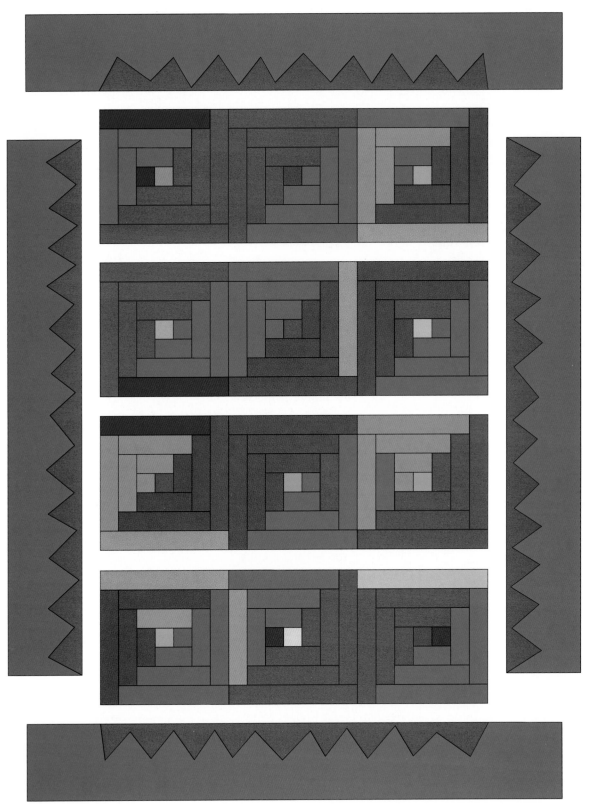

Quilt Assembly Diagram

Log Cabin Pillows

Materials

Extra Log Cabin blocks
Wool backing: 12¾" x 12¾" square
  per pillow
Buttons: as many as you like
Polyester stuffing

Photo by Kirstie McCormick

What do you do with extra blocks? Linda suggests making some cute pillows. You can too.

Finished block size: 12¼" x 12¼"

Finished pillow size: 12¼" x 12¼"

Pillow Assembly

1. Sew buttons to the Log Cabin block.

2. Place the pillow top and the pillow back right sides together.

3. Sew the pillow together, leaving 4" in the middle of one side open. Turn right side out. Press.

4. Lightly stuff the pillow with stuffing.

5. Hand stitch the opening closed.

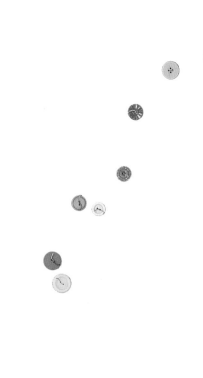

Wonderful Wooly Pincushions

Photo by Kirstie McCormick

Made by Becky Goldsmith, 2003
Finished pincushion sizes: 2"–3½"

It's so much fun to take little bits of colorful wool and make these cute pincushions. Whether you give them to your friends or pile them up next to your chair, you are going to enjoy them. Becky had to pry them away from her son Jeff—he wanted to juggle them! Sometimes your quilt shop will have wool on the bolt. Often you'll find squares of wool in various sizes. Most of these pincushions can be made from small scraps of wool.

Fuzzy Volcano Pincushion

Materials

Purple volcano body: 7" x 7" square
Lava tassel strips: small scraps of 4–6 different colors
Buttons: 11 buttons from ⅜"–⅝" in diameter
Embroidery floss
Polyester stuffing
Rice: ¼ cup or so

Cutting

Lava tassel strips
Cut 12 strips ⅜" x 3".

Volcano Pincushion Assembly

1. Make a template for the volcano using the pattern on page 18. If you want to make a slightly smaller volcano, reduce the template 85%.

2. Trace around the template on the wrong side of the wool. Cut out the fabric on the drawn line.

3. With wrong sides together, pin together the seams marked A on the pattern.

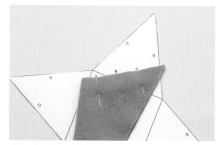

Pin the A sides together.

4. Beginning at the base of the pincushion, sew the seam using a blanket stitch with 3 strands of embroidery floss. Stop 1" away from the top. Knot the thread.

Sew to within 1" of the top and knot the thread.

5. Continue in this manner until all 4 sides are sewn together.

6. Spoon some rice into the pincushion to weight it. Stuff the pincushion firmly with polyester stuffing.

7. Group the lava tassel strips together. Arrange them so that they look nice. Tie the tassel tightly together ½" from one end.

Tie the ends of the lava strips together.

8. Insert the tied end of the lava tassel into the top of the pincushion. Sew through the pincushion and the tassel to hold the tassel in place.

Sew through the pincushion and the tassel.

9. Tightly wrap embroidery thread around the outside of the pincushion, cinching it around the tassel. Knot the thread.

Tightly wrap embroidery thread around the pincushion to hold the lava tassel in place.

10. Trim the ends of the lava strips at slightly different angles and lengths.

11. Sew buttons to the outside of the pincushion.

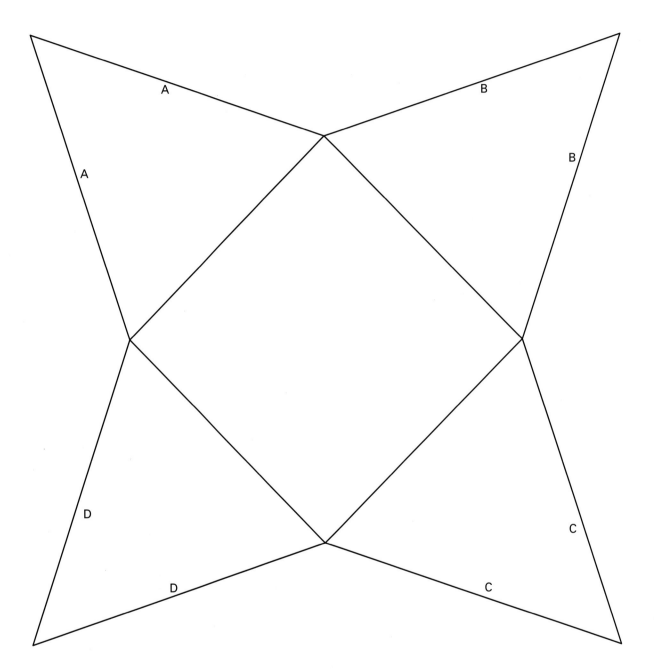

Volcano Pincushion Pattern

Curl Up Quilts

Cube Pincusion

Materials

Small scraps of red, teal, and green wool
Buttons: 2 buttons 1" in diameter
Polyester stuffing

Cutting

Red wool
Cut 2 squares 2½" x 2½".

Teal wool
Cut 2 squares 2½" x 2½".

Green wool
Cut 2 squares 2½" x 2½".

Cube Pincushion Assembly

1. Group wool squares together into the following pairs:
Red square with teal square
Red square with green square
Teal square with green square

2. Pin each pair of squares wrong sides together. Sew each pair together.

Use a scant ¼" seam. Begin and end a scant ¼" away from either end of all seams.

Sew pairs together.

3. Choose 2 pairs of squares. Keep like colors opposite each other across the cube. Pin one side together at a time and sew it.

Keep like colors opposite each other across the cube. Pin and sew together one side at a time.

4. Pin and sew the next side in the same manner.

Pin and sew the next side.

5. Position the last pair of squares in the cube. Work around the edges, pinning and sewing one seam at a time. **Do not sew the last seam.**

Work around the cube, pinning and sewing one seam at a time.

6. Before sewing the last seam, turn the cube right side out and stuff it firmly with polyester stuffing. Turn the seam allowances into the cube and invisibly stitch it shut.

7. Place buttons on opposite sides of the cube. Sew the buttons on through the cube and pull the thread tight to squash the pincushion a little bit.

Heart Pincushion

Materials

Small scraps of red, yellow, orange,
  and green wool
Embroidery floss in matching colors
Polyester stuffing

Heart Pincushion Assembly

1. Make templates using the patterns below.

2. Trace 2 hearts on the wrong side of the red wool. Cut out the hearts on the drawn line.

3. Trace the flower on the wrong side of the yellow wool. Cut it out with pinking shears if you want a pinked edge on the flower. Trace the flower center on orange wool and cut it out. Trace 2 leaves on green wool and cut them out.

4. Place the 2 leaves on the right side of a heart. Stitch down the center of the leaves with a running stitch.

5. Place the flower and flower center on the stitched leaves. Stitch them down with random straight stitches in the center of the flower.

6. Place the 2 hearts wrong sides together. Sew them together with a running stitch in matching thread. Leave an opening on the side to stuff the heart.

7. Stuff the heart. Sew the opening shut.

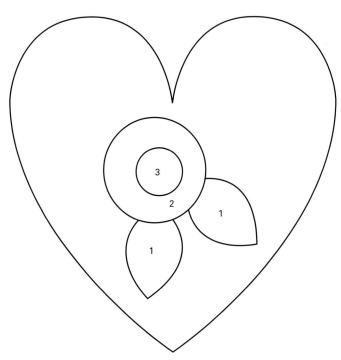

Heart Pincushion Pattern

Sushi Rolls Pincushions

Materials

Scraps at least 2" wide and 10"–20" long: blue, fuschia, lime, yellow, and green wool

Buttons: 6 buttons ⅜"–⅝" in diameter

These are fast, fun, and functional. Make bigger or smaller "sushi rolls" by cutting shorter or fewer strips. Use your imagination and embellish them to your heart's delight.

Cutting

Blue wool
Cut 1 strip 2" x 20".

Fuchsia wool
Cut 1 strip 2" x 16".

Lime wool
Cut 1 strip 2" x 14".

Yellow wool
Cut 1 strip 2" x 12".

Green wool
Cut 1 strip 2" x 10".

Sushi Roll Pincushion Assembly

1. Work on top of a cutting mat. Place the blue strip wrong side up on the mat.

2. Place the fuchsia strip on top of the blue strip. Offset the end by ⅜".

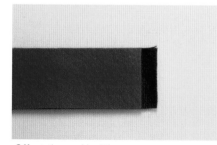

Offset the end by ⅜".

3. Continue in this manner, placing the next longest strip on the stack. Offset the end of each strip by ⅜". Be careful to keep the long edges aligned.

Continue stacking strips, offsetting the end of each strip by ⅜".

4. Begin rolling the strips at the "offset" end. Take it slow. Keep the long edges even. Make sure to keep the roll tight. As you roll, the strips will bunch up. Take a moment and smooth out the wool as you roll.

Smooth out the wool as you roll.

5. When you reach the end of the roll, use 3 long pins to secure the roll. Use a matching or contrasting floss to sew the end of the outermost wool strip in place.

Sew the end of the outermost strip in place.

6. Cut accent circles of wool to go behind the buttons. They don't have to be perfectly round, but they do need to be bigger than the buttons.

7. Sew the wool accent circles and buttons around the outside of the sushi roll pincushion.

Stacked Squares Pincushion

Materials

Scraps of at least **12 different wools in rainbow colors**

Buttons: 8 yellow buttons ⅜"–½" in diameter and 8 black/white buttons ⅜"–½" in diameter

Perle cotton

Cutting

Cut 1 square 3" x 3" from at least 12 different colors of wool.

These are fast, easy, and they really, really work! We especially like how well this pincushion stays put on the arm of a chair.

Stacked Squares Pincushion Assembly

1. Neatly stack the squares.

2. Begin in a corner. With a button above and a button below, sew the stacks tightly together. Use a double strand of perle cotton. Tie a square knot above the button on one side of the pincushion. Cut the perle cotton leaving ¼" tails of thread.

Sew the stack together with a button above and below. Tie off with a square knot.

3. Continue in this manner, sewing the corners first, then the sides.

Sunny Days

Made by Linda Jenkins, 2003

Finished appliqué block size: 9" x 9"

Finished quilt size: 54" x 69"

Isn't this the happiest quilt you've ever seen? Linda made this quilt for her favorite (and only) sister Judy who has the sunniest disposition you can imagine. This quilt is absolutely perfect for her.

Materials

This is a scrappy quilt. Use the yardage amounts below as a guide. They will vary with the number of fabrics you use.

Light yellow solid block backgrounds, top and
  bottom borders: 2¾ yards
Lighter yellow scrappy Nine-Patches and side border
  triangle squares: a variety to total 1⅓ yards
Darker yellow scrappy Nine-Patches and side border
  triangle squares: a variety to total 1¼ yards
Striped inner border, top and bottom borders,
  binding: 1⅞ yards
Appliqué: A wide variety of fabric scraps for flowers,
  leaves, stems, and bottom border circles
Backing and sleeve: 4¼ yards
Batting: 58" x 73" (we used Warm & Natural Cotton)

Cutting

Light yellow solid fabric
Top border background: Cut 1 strip (lengthwise)
  6" x 56".
Appliqué block backgrounds: Cut 15 squares 11" x 11".
Bottom border triangle-squares: Cut 4 squares 8" x 8",
  then cut each in half diagonally.

Lighter yellow fabrics
Scrappy Nine-Patches: Cut 75 squares 3½" x 3½" **or** if you
  prefer to strip-piece the Nine-Patches: Cut 8 strips
  3½" x 40".
Side border triangle-squares: Cut 42 squares 3½" x 3½".

Darker yellow fabrics
Scrappy Nine-Patches: Cut 60 squares 3½" x 3½" **or** if you
  prefer to strip-piece the Nine-Patches: Cut 7 strips
  3½" x 40".
Side border triangle-squares: Cut 42 squares 3½" x 3½".

Striped fabric
*Measure your quilt top and outer borders before cutting
  the inner borders.*
Inner border: Cut 8 strips 2" x 40".
Bottom border: Cut 4 squares 8" x 8", then cut each in
  half diagonally.
Binding: Cut 1 square 31" x 31" to make 3"-wide
  continuous bias binding 260" long. (Refer to pages
  71–72 for instructions.)

Cut fabric for appliqué as needed.

Block and Border Assembly

Refer to pages 66–68 for instructions on making the positioning overlay and preparing the appliqué. Appliqué patterns for this project are on the pullout pattern sheet at the back of the book.

Appliqué Tips

Use the *cutaway appliqué* technique for the stems and leaves. Use the *circle appliqué* technique for the round flower parts. (Refer to pages 69–70 for instructions.)

Appliqué Blocks

1. The flower on each appliqué block is randomly placed. Keep the appliqué pieces at least 1¼" from each edge of the background block. Do not let the appliqué wander into the seamline. Flower blocks #1, #2, and #5 are each used 3 times each in this quilt. Flower blocks #3, #4 and #6 are each used 2 times each in this quilt.

2. After the appliqué is complete, gently press the blocks on the wrong side. Trim each block to 9½" x 9½" square.

Nine-Patch Blocks

Refer to page 75 if you prefer to strip-piece your Nine-Patch blocks.

1. For a scrappier mix of fabrics, arrange the 75 lighter and 60 darker squares on your design wall. Linda generally kept the lighter squares in the corners and center of each block.

2. To make each block, sew the squares together into rows. Press toward the darker fabric. Sew the rows together to make 15 blocks. Press.

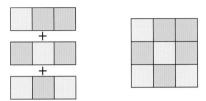

Make scrappy Nine-Patches.

Side Borders

Refer to page 76 for instructions on how to make triangle-squares.

1. Combine one lighter yellow 3½" square with one darker yellow 3½" square for each triangle-square. Be very careful when you press. Do not stretch the triangle-squares. Linda suggests you might want to finger-press them instead of ironing.

2. Make 42 triangle-squares.

Bottom Border

1. Sew one light yellow solid triangle to one striped triangle on the diagonal. Be careful not to stretch this diagonal seam. Press gently.

2. Make 8 triangle-squares.

3. Appliqué a border circle in the center of each triangle-square. Press.

4. After the appliqué is complete, gently press the blocks on the wrong side. Trim the block to 6½" x 6½".

Top Border

1. Press the light yellow background border strip in half horizontally and vertically.

2. Appliqué 12 striped border circles to the background. The centers of adjacent circles are 4⅜" apart. Make sure the stripes in the circles run in the same direction. Linda's are vertical.

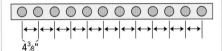

4⅜"

Place the circles on the background 4⅜" apart, from circle center to circle center.

3. After the appliqué is complete, gently press the border on the wrong side.

Quilt Assembly

Refer to the Quilt Assembly Diagram for quilt construction.

Refer to Borders on page 8 for instructions on measuring your quilt top and cutting borders to size as needed.

1. Put the flower blocks and Nine-Patches on your design wall. Move them around until you are happy with their placement.

2. Sew the blocks together into rows. Press the seams in alternate directions so they nest when the rows are sewn together. Make 6 rows.

3. Sew the rows together. Press the seams toward the bottom of the quilt.

4. Put the quilt on your design wall. Arrange the bottom border triangles. When you are happy with their placement, sew the 8 triangle-squares together. Press the seams toward the darker fabric.

5. Arrange the side border triangles. When you are happy with their placement, sew 21 triangle-squares together for each side border. Press the seams toward the darker fabric.

6. Measure the height of the quilt top and the side triangle borders. If your quilt top or pieced borders are a different size from those listed in the cutting instructions, you will need to adjust the inner border length or width. Cut the striped side inner borders as needed and sew to the sides of the quilt. Press toward the inner border.

7. Measure the width of the quilt top and the top and bottom appliqué borders. Adjust and cut the striped top and bottom inner borders as needed and sew to the top and bottom of the quilt. Press toward the inner border.

8. Sew the side triangle borders to the quilt. Press toward the inner border.

9. Sew the top and bottom appliqué borders to the quilt. Press toward the inner border.

10. Finish the quilt. (Refer to page 68 for instructions.)

Quilt Assembly Diagram

Curl-Up Quilts

Meow & Woof

Made by Linda Jenkins, 2003

Finished appliqué block size: 15" x 15"

Finished quilt size: 45" x 60"

Linda made this quilt for her niece, Magen, who loves dogs and cats. Now Magen can cuddle up with her quilt and her pets!

Materials

This is a scrappy quilt. Use the yardage amounts below as a guide. They will vary with the number of fabrics you use.

Lighter black-and-white prints for block backgrounds, Four-Patches, checkerboard borders, and top and bottom borders: 2 yards

Darker black-and-white prints for Four-Patches, inner borders, checkerboard borders, and top and bottom borders: 1⅞ yards

Appliqué: A wide variety of fabric scraps

Black-and-white binding: 1 yard

Backing and sleeve: 3¾ yards

Batting: 49" x 64" (We used Warm & Natural Cotton)

Embroidery floss: for the whiskers

Permanent black gel pen: for the pupils of the eyes

Cutting

Lighter black-and-white prints

Appliqué block backgrounds: Cut 4 squares 17" x 17".

Four-Patches for the checkerboard border: Cut 6 strips 3" x 40".

Top and bottom border squares: Cut 9 squares 5½" x 5½".

Darker black-and-white prints

Measure your quilt top and outer borders before cutting the inner borders.

Inner side borders: Cut 2 strips 3" x 40½".

Inner top and bottom borders: Cut 2 strips 3" x 30½".

Meow & Woof border background: Cut 1 strip 7" x 32".

Four-Patches for the checkerboard border: Cut 6 strips 3" x 40".

Top and bottom border squares: Cut 9 squares 5½" x 5½".

Binding fabric

Cut 1 square 31" x 31" to make 3"-wide continuous bias binding 225" long. (Refer to pages 71–72 for instructions.)

Cut fabric for appliqué as needed.

meow • woof • meow • woof

Block and Border Assembly

Refer to pages 65–68 for instructions on making the positioning overlay and preparing the appliqué.

Enlarge patterns 200% before making templates and positioning overlay.

Appliqué Tips

Use the *cutaway appliqué* technique for the legs and words "meow" and "woof." Use the *circle appliqué* technique for the eyes and noses. (Refer to pages 69–70 for instructions.)

Appliqué Blocks

1. Appliqué the dog and cat blocks. Paint the pupils in the eyes with a permanent black gel pen. Heat set the eyes before appliquéing them to the blocks.

2. Embroider the whiskers using a stem stitch with 2 strands of floss.

3. After the appliqué is complete, gently press the blocks on the wrong side. Trim each block to 15½" x 15½".

4. Appliqué the Meow & Woof border.

5. After the appliqué is complete, gently press the border on the wrong side. Trim the border to 5½" x 30½".

Four-Patch Blocks for the Checkerboard Border

Refer to page 75 for strip-piecing instructions.

1. Sew the 6 light and 6 dark 3" x 40" strips together.

2. Cut 68 units 3" wide.

3. Make 34 Four-Patches.

Quilt Assembly

Refer to the Quilt Assembly Diagram for quilt construction.

Refer to Borders on page 8 for instructions on measuring your quilt top and cutting borders to size as needed.

1. Sew the 4 appliqué blocks together. Press the seams in alternate directions.

2. Sew the Meow & Woof border to the bottom of the quilt top. Press toward the border.

3. Sew 7 Four-Patches together for the top checkerboard border. Press. Repeat for the bottom checkerboard border.

4. Sew 10 Four-Patches together for each side checkerboard border. Press.

5. Measure the width of the quilt top and the checkerboard top and bottom borders. Adjust if necessary and cut the top and bottom inner borders as needed and sew to the top and bottom of the quilt. Press toward the inner border.

6. Measure the height of the quilt top and the checkerboard side borders. Adjust if necessary and cut the side inner borders as needed and sew to the sides of the quilt. Press toward the inner border.

7. Sew the top and bottom checkerboard borders to the quilt. Press toward the inner border.

8. Sew the side checkerboard borders to the quilt. Press toward the inner border.

9. Sew 5 dark and 4 light 5½" x 5½" squares together in a row for the top border. Sew it to the quilt. Press toward the outer border.

10. Sew 5 light and 4 dark 5½" x 5½" squares together in a row for the bottom border. Sew it to the quilt. Press toward the outer border.

11. Finish the quilt. (Refer to page 68 for instructions.)

Quilt Assembly Diagram

Woof Block #1
Enlarge 200%.

Curl-Up Quilts

Woof Block #2
Enlarge 200%.

Meow Block #3
Enlarge 200%.

Curl-Up Quilts

Meow Block #4
Enlarge 200%.

Meow Woof Border
Enlarge 200%.

Fruit Trees

Made by Linda Jenkins, 2003

Finished appliqué block size: 16" x 20"

Finished quilt size: 46¼" x 54¼"

These fruit trees have a warm, folk-art feeling that is hard to beat. The scrappy, neutral backgrounds and the colored accent strips in the border keep all attention focused on the trees themselves.

Materials

This is a scrappy quilt. Use the yardage amounts below as a guide. They will vary with the number of fabrics you use.

Light neutral prints for block backgrounds and borders: 2½ yards

Appliqué, scrappy sashing, and binding: A wide variety of fabric scraps to total 1½ yards

Backing and sleeve: 3½ yards

Batting: 51" x 59" (We used Hobbs Organic Cotton)

Cutting

Light neutral prints

Appliqué block backgrounds: Cut 16 rectangles 10" x 12".
Border: Cut many strips of random lengths ranging from 2"–9" long and 6½" wide. (31 were used in the quilt pictured.)

Scrappy sashing fabrics

A: Cut 2 strips 1¼" x 16½".
B: Cut 3 strips 1¼" x 21¼".
C: Cut 4 strips 1¼" x 16½".
D: Cut 3 strips 1¼" x 22".

Binding fabric

Cut 3"-wide strips of varying lengths on the bias from a variety of colorful fabrics to make scrappy bias binding 225" long. (Refer to pages 72–73 for instructions.)

Appliqué fabrics

Cut fabric for appliqué as needed.

Cut border accent color strips 1" x 6½" from the appliqué fabric. (17 were used in the quilt pictured.)

Block and Border Assembly

Appliqué Blocks

Refer to pages 65–68 for instructions on making the positioning overlay and preparing the appliqué.

Enlarge patterns 200% before making templates and positioning overlay.

> **Appliqué Tips**
>
> Use the *cutaway appliqué* technique for the branches. Use the *circle appliqué* technique for the fruit. (Refer to pages 69–70 for instructions.)

1. Place the 10" x 12" background rectangles on your design wall. Move them around until you are happy with their placement. Sew 4 rectangles together for each block. Press.

2. Appliqué the blocks.

3. After the appliqué is complete, gently press the blocks on the wrong side. Trim each block to 16½" x 20½".

Borders

In true quilting tradition, Linda used the fabric she had available for the borders. There is no pattern; the fabric strips that make up the border are random lengths.

1. Place your blocks and sashing on your design wall.

2. Arrange the 6½" wide pieces of border fabric around the edges of the quilt. Insert the 1" x 6½" accent strips sparingly.

3. When you are happy with the arrangement, sew the border strips together.

Quilt Assembly

Refer to the Quilt Assembly Diagram for quilt construction.

Refer to Borders on page 8 for instructions on measuring your quilt top and cutting sashing and borders to size as needed.

1. Sew an A sashing to the top of the Apple Tree and the Lemon Tree blocks. Press toward the sashing.

2. Sew a B sashing between the Apple Tree and the Lemon Tree blocks and on each side of these blocks. Press toward the sashing.

3. Sew a C sashing to the top and bottom of the Orange Tree and Cherry Tree blocks. Press toward the sashing.

4. Sew a D sashing between the Orange Tree and Cherry Tree blocks and on each side of these blocks. Press toward the sashing.

5. Sew the rows of appliqué blocks together. Press toward the sashing.

6. Trim the top and bottom borders to 6½" x 34¾". Sew the borders to the quilt. Press toward the sashing.

7. Trim the side borders to 6½" x 54¾". Sew the borders to the quilt. Press toward the sashing.

8. Finish the quilt. (Refer to page 68 for instructions.)

Quilt Assembly Diagram

Apple Tree
Enlarge 200%.

Lemon Tree
Enlarge 200%.

Curl-Up Quilts

Orange Tree
Enlarge 200%.

Cherry Tree
Enlarge 200%.

Fruit Trees

Firecracker Garden

Made by Becky Goldsmith, 2003

Finished appliqué block size: 16" x 16"

Finished quilt size: 48" x 60"

With flannel flowers the colors of the 4th of July, this quilt brings summer and winter together!

Materials

This is a scrappy quilt. Use the yardage amounts below as a guide. They will vary with the number of fabrics you use.

Off-white solid block backgrounds: 1⅛ yards

Off-white print appliqué border backgrounds and pieced border: 1¼ yards

Red #1 appliqué and Nine-Patches: 1⅓ yards

Red #2 appliqué and Nine-Patches: 1⅛ yards

Blue solid flower centers and inner border: ¾ yard

Appliqué: A variety of blue, brown, green, and yellow fabric scraps for flowers, leaves, and stems

Red binding: A variety of red fabric scraps to total ¾ yard

Backing and sleeve: 4¼ yards

Batting: 52" x 64" (We used off-white cotton flannel)

Cutting

Off-white solid fabric

Appliqué block backgrounds: Cut 4 squares 18" x 18".

Off-white print fabric

Top border background: Cut 1 strip 10" x 34".

Bottom border background: Cut 1 strip 6" x 34".

Nine-Patches: Cut 144 squares 2½" x 2½" *or* if you prefer to strip-piece the Nine-Patches: Cut 9 strips 2½" x 40", then cut into 18 strips 20" long.

Red fabrics

Nine-Patches: Cut 144 squares 2½" x 2½" *or* if you prefer to strip-piece the Nine-Patches: Cut 9 strips 2½" x 40", then cut into 18 strips 20" long.

Use the remaining red fabric in the appliqué.

Blue solid fabric

Measure your quilt top and outer borders before cutting the inner borders.

Side inner borders: Cut 3 strips 2½" x 40", seam them together end-to-end, and cut 2 strips 2½" x 48½".

Top and bottom inner borders: Cut 2 strips 2½" x 36½".

Use the remaining blue fabric in the appliqué.

Binding fabrics

Cut 3" wide strips of varying lengths on the bias from a variety of red plaid fabrics to make scrappy bias binding 230" long. (Refer to pages 72–73 for instructions.)

Cut fabric for appliqué as needed.

Block and Border Assembly

Refer to pages 65–68 for instructions on making the positioning overlay and preparing the appliqué. **The appliqué patterns are at the back of the book on the pullout.**

Appliqué Tips

Use the *cutaway appliqué* technique for the stems and leaves. Use the *circle appliqué* technique for the round flower parts. (Refer to pages 69–70 for instructions.)

Appliqué Blocks

1. Appliqué 4 Firecracker Flower blocks.

2. After the appliqué is complete, gently press the blocks on the wrong side. Trim each block to 16½" x 16½" square.

Top Appliqué Border

1. Appliqué the top border. Space the flowers as indicated below.

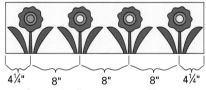

4¼"　8"　8"　8"　4¼"
Space the flower centers 8" apart.

2. After the appliqué is complete, gently press the border on the wrong side.

Bottom Appliqué Border

1. Appliqué the bottom border. Space the flowers as indicated below.

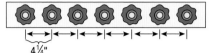

4¼"
Space the flower centers 4¼" apart.

2. After the appliqué is complete, gently press the border on the wrong side.

Nine-Patch Blocks

Refer to page 75 if you prefer to strip-piece your Nine-Patch blocks.
1. For a scrappier mix of fabrics, arrange the 144 off-white squares and 144 red squares on your design wall. Arrange 16 light Nine-Patches made from 5 off-white squares and 4 red squares and 16 dark Nine-Patches made from 4 off-white squares and 5 red squares.

2. To make each block, sew the squares together into rows. Press toward the darker fabric. Sew the rows together to make 16 light Nine-Patches and 16 dark Nine-Patches. Press.

Quilt Assembly

Refer to the Quilt Assembly Diagram for quilt construction.

Refer to Borders on page 8 for instructions on measuring your quilt top and cutting borders to size as needed.

1. Sew the Firecracker Flower blocks together into rows. Press the seams in alternate directions so they nest when the rows are sewn together.

2. Sew the rows together. Press the seams toward the bottom of the quilt.

3. Trim the top appliqué border to 8½" x the measured width of the quilt top. Sew the border to the quilt. Press toward the blocks.

4. Trim the bottom appliqué border to 4½" x the measured width of the quilt top. Sew the border to the quilt. Press toward the blocks.

5. Sew 4 light and 4 dark Nine-Patches together for each side border, alternating light and dark Nine-Patches.

6. Sew 4 light and 4 dark Nine-Patches together for the top and bottom borders, alternating light and dark Nine-Patches.

7. Measure the height of the quilt top and the Nine-Patch side borders. If your quilt top or pieced borders are a different size than those listed in the cutting instructions, you will need to adjust the inner border length or width. Cut the blue side inner borders as needed and sew to the sides of the quilt. Press toward the inner border.

8. Measure the width of the quilt top and the Nine-Patch top and bottom borders. Cut the blue top and bottom inner borders as needed and sew to the top and bottom of the quilt. Press toward the inner border.

9. Sew the Nine-Patch side borders to the sides of the quilt. Press toward the inner border.

10. Sew the Nine-Patch top and bottom borders to the quilt. Press toward the inner border.

Using Flannel as Batting

Becky lives in Texas where it is warm much of the year. She wanted to see how cotton flannel would work as a batting. The answer is, it worked pretty well. It is just a little lighter than cotton batting, has a low loft, and was easy to machine quilt.

If your quilt is wider than the flannel, piece it as you would a backing. Press the seams open to cut down on bulk. Make sure that the seams in the flannel batting and the seams in your backing are offset.

11. Finish the quilt. (Refer to page 68 for instructions.)

Quilt Assembly Diagram

Sweet Pea

Made by Becky Goldsmith, 2003
Finished appliqué block size: 25" x 30"
Finished quilt size: 35" x 41"

Becky made this quilt for her granddaughter, Elanor, whom she calls "Sweet Pea." After raising two boys it's nice to work with pink! This is a fast quilt to make, and it is just the right size for your Sweet Pea.

Materials

Pink-and-white gingham check block background: ⅞ yard

Light blue stripe inner border: ½ yard

Dark pink wavy inner border: ½ yard

Green, pink, and white plaid outer border: ⅝ yard

Appliqué: A variety of pink, yellow, and green fabric scraps for flowers and leaves

Green-and-white plaid stems and binding: 1⅛ yards

Perle cotton for fronds

Backing and sleeve: 1¾ yards

Batting: 39" x 45" (We used Hobbs Organic Cotton)

Cutting

Pink-and-white gingham fabric

Appliqué block background: Cut 1 rectangle 27" x 32".

Light blue stripe fabric

Side inner borders: Cut 2 strips 3" x 30½".

Top and bottom inner borders: Cut 2 strips 3" x 30½".

Dark pink fabric

Wavy side inner borders: Cut 2 strips 3" x 35½".

Wavy top and bottom inner borders: Cut 2 strips 3" x 30½".

Green, pink, and white plaid fabric

Side borders: Cut 2 strips 3½" x 34½".

Top border: Cut 1 strip 3½" x 35½".

Bottom border: Cut 1 strip 6" x 37" (will be trimmed after appliqué).

Green-and-white plaid fabric

Binding: Cut 1 square 26" x 26" to make 3"-wide continuous bias binding 162" long. (Refer to pages 71–72 for instructions.)

Use the remaining fabric for the stems.

Cut fabric for appliqué as needed.

Block and Border Assembly

Refer to pages 65–68 for instructions on making the positioning overlay and preparing the appliqué. **Appliqué patterns for this project are on the pullout pattern sheet at the back of the book.**

Appliqué Tips

Use the *cutaway appliqué* technique for the stems, bases of the flowers, and letters. (Refer to page 69 for instructions.)

Appliqué Block

1. Appliqué the Sweet Pea block.

2. Place the block over the pattern. Lightly trace the frond lines onto the background fabric.

3. Embroider the fronds with perle cotton in a straight stitch.

4. After the appliqué and embroidery are complete, gently press the block on the wrong side. Trim it to 25½" x 30½".

Appliqué the Inner Border

Refer to Borders on page 8 for instructions on measuring your quilt top and cutting borders to size as needed.

1. Sew the blue side inner borders to the quilt. Press toward the inner border.

2. Sew the blue top and bottom inner borders to the quilt. Press toward the inner border.

3. Cut a dark pink side border. Place it on a cutting mat and use a rotary cutter to cut a gently waving curve down one long side. The difference between the height of the "peaks" and the depth of the "valleys" of the curves should not be much more than ¼".

4. Finger-press a ³⁄₁₆" turn-under allowance along the curved edge of the strip. Place the curved edge of the strip on one side of the quilt over the blue striped border. Allow ¼"–¾" of the blue to show. The 2 inner borders combined will have a finished width of 2".

5. Baste, then appliqué the strip in place.

6. Repeat Steps 3–5 for the other side border.

7. Repeat Steps 3–5 for the top and bottom borders.

8. Turn the quilt over. Trim away the excess blue striped fabric, leaving a ¼" seam allowance.

9. Use rotary tools and trim the combined inner borders to 2¼" wide.

Bottom Sweet Pea Appliqué Border

1. Appliqué the bottom Sweet Pea border.

2. After the appliqué is complete, gently press the border on the wrong side.

Quilt Assembly

Refer to the Quilt Assembly Diagram for quilt construction.

Refer to Borders on page 8 for instructions on measuring your quilt top and cutting borders to size as needed.

1. Sew the side outer borders to the quilt. Press the seams toward the outer border.

2. Sew the top outer border to the quilt. Press toward the outer border.

3. Trim the bottom Sweet Pea appliqué border to 4½" x 35½". Sew the Sweet Pea border to the quilt. Press toward the appliqué border.

4. Finish the quilt. (Refer to page 68 for instructions.)

Quilt Assembly Diagram

May Baskets

Made by Becky Goldsmith, 2003

Finished appliqué block sizes:

   10" x 15" and 15" x 15"

Finished quilt size: 38" x 43"

Do you remember the tradition of leaving a basket of flowers hanging on your mom's front door on May Day? Becky does! When she was a little girl, she'd hang the May basket on her own doorknob, ring the bell, and hide until her mom came to find it. These festive flowers remind her of those special memories.

Materials

The borders in this quilt are scrappy. Use the yardage amount below as a guide.

Brown-and-gold plaid background and some border: 1 yard

Darker brown plaid sashing: ⅜ yard

Brown border backgrounds: assorted fabric scraps to total 1¼ yards

Purple-and-green stripe for the baskets: ¾ yard

Purple solid basket trim: ⅜ yard

Appliqué: A wide variety of fabric scraps

Dark brown striped binding: ⅞ yard

Backing and sleeve: 2⅞ yards

Batting: 42" x 47" (We used Warm & Natural Cotton)

Cutting

Brown-and-gold plaid fabric appliqué block backgrounds: Cut 2 squares 17" x 17" and 2 rectangles 12" x 17".

Darker brown plaid sashing fabric:
A: Cut 2 strips 1½" x 15½".
B: Cut 3 strips 1½" x 26½".
C: Cut 2 strips 1½" x 33½".

Border Fabrics: Cut strips of random length 7" wide from the remaining brown fabrics and piece together to total 168" long. (6 fabrics ranging from 5"–9" were used in the quilt pictured.)

Dark brown striped fabric binding: Cut 1 square 26" x 26" to make 3"-wide continuous bias binding 175" long. (Refer to pages 71–72 for instructions.)

Cut fabric for appliqué as needed.

Block and Border Assembly

Appliqué Blocks

Refer to pages 65–68 for instructions on making the positioning overlay and preparing the appliqué.

Enlarge patterns 200% before making templates and positioning overlay.

> **Appliqué Tips**
>
> Use the *cutaway appliqué* technique for the basket handles and stems. Use the *circle appliqué* technique for the flower centers. (Refer to pages 69–70 for instructions.)

1. Appliqué the basket blocks.

2. After the appliqué is complete, gently press the blocks on the wrong side. Trim blocks #1 and #4 to 15½" x 15½". Trim blocks #2 and #3 to 10½" x 15½".

Borders

In true quilting tradition, Becky used the fabric she had for the borders. There is no pattern; the fabric strips that make up the borders are random lengths.

1. Place the blocks and sashing on your design wall.

2. Arrange the 7"-wide pieces of border fabric around the edges of the quilt. Move them around until you are happy with their placement.

3. Sew the border strips together.

4. Make the side borders 7" x 45".

5. Make the top and bottom borders 7" x 30".

6. Appliqué the flowers onto the borders. The flower centers are 4⅝" apart on all borders. Always position the center flowers first.

The flower centers are 4⅝" apart on all borders.

7. When the appliqué is complete, press the borders on the wrong side.

Quilt Assembly

Refer to the Quilt Assembly Diagram for quilt construction.

Refer to Borders on page 8 for instructions on measuring your quilt top and cutting sashing and borders to size as needed.

1. Sew an A sashing between block #1 and block #2. Press toward the sashing.

2. Sew an A sashing between block #3 and block #4. Press toward the sashing.

3. Sew the B sashings to the rows of appliqué blocks. Press toward the sashing.

4. Sew the C sashings to each side of the quilt. Press toward the sashing.

5. Trim the top and bottom appliqué borders to 5½" x 28½". Sew the borders to the quilt. Press toward the border.

6. Trim the side appliqué borders to 5½" x 43½". Sew the borders to the quilt. Press toward the border.

7. Finish the quilt. (Refer to page 68 for instructions.)

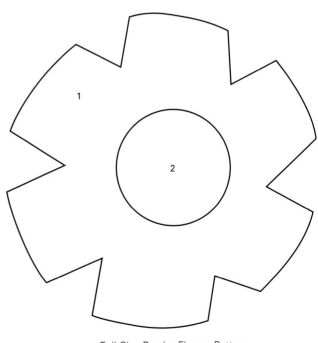

Full Size Border Flower Pattern

Quilt Assembly Diagram

Basket Block #1
Enlarge 200%.

Curl-Up Quilts

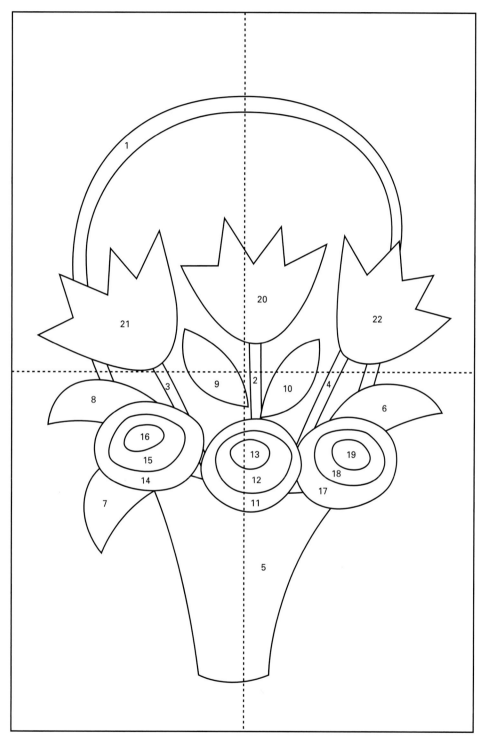

Basket Block #2
Enlarge 200%.

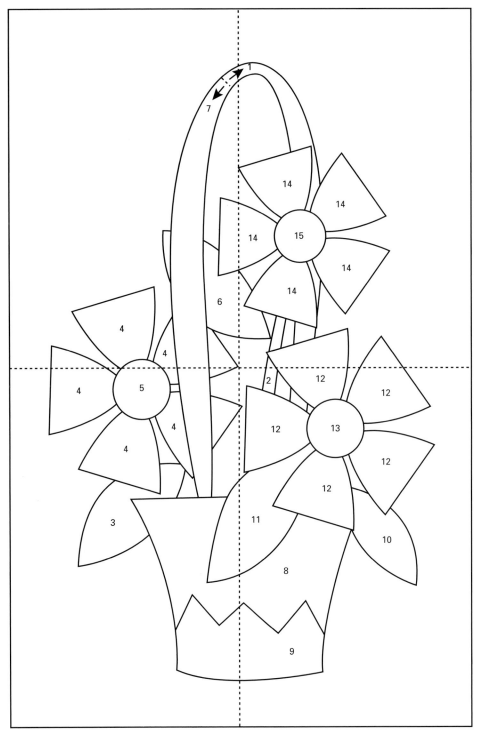

Basket Block #3
Enlarge 200%.

Basket Block #4
Enlarge 200%.

Pillows

Photo by Kirstie McCormick and Diane Pedersen

Made by Becky Goldsmith, 2003

Don't you just love the way pillows dress up a room? Flannel pillows are cozy and cuddly. Becky made these three pillows to go in her yellow bedroom.

Happy Cat Pillow

Finished appliqué block size: 12" x 12"

Finished pillow size: 16" x 16"

Materials

Yellow block background: ½ yard or a fat quarter

Green border: ¼ yard

Appliqué: A variety of fabric scraps

Yellow backing: ⅝ yard

Embroidery floss: for the whiskers and mouth

Permanent black gel pen: for the pupils of the eyes

Pillow form: 16" x 16"

Cutting

Yellow background fabric

Appliqué block background: Cut 1 square 14" x 14".

Green fabric

Side borders: Cut 2 strips 2½" x 12½".

Top and bottom borders: Cut 2 strips 2½" x 16½".

Yellow backing fabric

Backing: Cut 2 rectangles 16½" x 12".

Cut fabric for appliqué as needed.

Block Assembly

Appliqué the Block

Refer to pages 65–68 for instructions on making the positioning overlay and preparing the appliqué.

Appliqué Tip

Use the *cutaway appliqué* technique for the body of the cat. (Refer to page 69 for instructions.)

---

1. Use block #4 from *Meow & Woof* (pattern is on page 33) and reduce it to 80% of the original size.

2. Appliqué the block. Draw the pupils in the eyes with a permanent black gel pen. Heat set the eyes before appliquéing them to the blocks.

3. Embroider the whiskers and mouth using a straight stitch with 2 strands of embroidery floss.

4. After the appliqué and embroidery are complete, gently press the block on the wrong side. Trim it to 12½" x 12½".

Pillow Assembly

Refer to the Pillow Assembly Diagram

1. Sew the side borders to the block. Press the seams toward the border.

2. Sew the top and bottom borders to the block. Press toward the border.

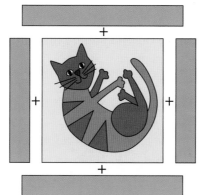

Attach the Borders.

3. Turn under and hem one long side of each of the pillow back rectangles.

4. Place the pillow back rectangles and the pillow top right sides together. Overlap the hemmed edges of the pillow backs so that the raw edges are even with the edges of the pillow top.

5. Sew the pillow top and back together. Turn right side out. Press.

6. Top stitch the outer edges of the pillow to ³⁄₁₆" from the edge.

7. Insert the pillow form.

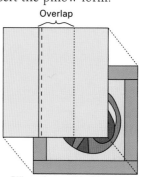

Pillow Assembly Diagram

Sunny Days Pillow

Finished pillow size: 13" x 18"

Materials

Yellow background: ⅝ yard
Appliqué: A variety of fabric scraps
Buttons: 10 decorative 1" buttons
Pillow form 13" x 18" or
 polyester stuffing

Cutting

Yellow fabric
Pillow top: Cut 1 rectangle 15" x 24½".
Pillow back: Cut 1 rectangle 13½" x 24½".

Cut fabric for appliqué as needed.

Pillow Top and Back Assembly

Hem the Ends

1. Turn under each short side of the 2 rectangles ¼". Press.

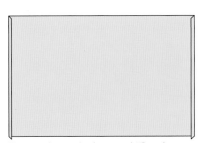

Turn under each short end ¼" and press.

2. Turn under an additional 2" to create a hem at each end of the 2 rectangles. Sew the hems in place.

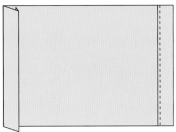

Turn under an additional 2" at each short end, press, and sew.

Appliqué the Block

Refer to pages 65–68 for instructions on making the positioning overlay and preparing the appliqué.

> ### Appliqué Tip
> Use the *cutaway appliqué* technique for the leaves and stems. (Refer to page 69 for instructions.)

1. Use block #1 and block #6 from *Sunny Days* (patterns are on the pullout at the back of the book) on the larger rectangle. Be sure to position the flowers so they are inside the hems and at least 2" from the top and bottom edges of the pillow front.

Position the flowers inside the hem and at least 2" from the top and bottom of the pillow front.

2. Appliqué the pillow top.

3. After the appliqué is complete, gently press the pillow top on the wrong side. Make sure the appliqué is centered, then trim the pillow top to 13½" wide.

Pillow Assembly

1. Place the pillow front and back right sides together. Sew them together along the top and bottom raw edges.

2. Turn the pillow right side out. Press.

3. Insert the pillow form. Pin the open sides together. Sew the sides closed with buttons.

Close the open sides with buttons.

Tossed Flowers Pillow

Finished appliqué block size: 14" x 14"

Finished pillow size: 14" x 14"

Materials

Yellow block background: ½ yard or a fat quarter
Appliqué: A variety of fabric scraps
Yellow backing: ½ yard
Red pompom trim: 2 yards
Pillow form: 14" x 14"

Cutting

Yellow background fabric
Appliqué block background: Cut 1 square 16" x 16".

Yellow backing fabric
Backing: Cut 2 rectangles 14½" x 10".

Cut fabric for appliqué as needed.

Block Assembly
Appliqué the Block

Refer to pages 65–68 for instructions on making the positioning overlay and preparing the appliqué.

> ### Appliqué Tip
> Use the *circle appliqué* technique for the flower centers. (Refer to page 70 for instructions.)

1. Use the flowers and leaves from *May Baskets*, block #3 (pattern is on page 56).

2. Scatter the flowers and leaves on the pillow top. Keep them at least 2" away from outer edges.

3. Appliqué the block.

4. After the appliqué is complete, gently press the block on the wrong side. Trim it to 14½" x 14½".

Pillow Assembly

Refer to the Pillow Assembly Diagram on page 59 for the **Happy Cat Pillow.**

1. Baste the pompom trim to the outer edges of the pillow top. Be sure that only the decorative portion of the trim will show when the pillow is turned.

2. Turn under and hem one long side of each of the pillow back rectangles.

3. Place the pillow back rectangles and the pillow top right sides together. Overlap the hemmed edges of the pillow backs so that the raw edges are even with the edges of the pillow top.

4. Sew the pillow together. Turn right side out. Press.

5. Insert the pillow form.

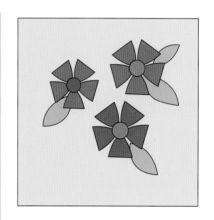

General Appliqué Instructions

We have a great way to do appliqué using sturdy laminated appliqué templates and a clear vinyl positioning overlay that makes it a snap to position all the pieces. If you're new to Piece O' Cake Designs appliqué techniques, read through all of these instructions before beginning a project.

For a more complete description of all our appliqué techniques, refer to our book *The Appliqué Sampler*.

Preparing the Backgrounds for Appliqué

Always cut the background fabric larger than the size it will be when it is pieced into the quilt. The outer edges of the block can stretch and fray as you handle it while stitching. The appliqué can shift during stitching and cause the block to shrink slightly. For these reasons it is best to add 1" to all sides of the backgrounds when you cut them out. We have included this amount in the cutting instructions for each quilt. You will trim the blocks to size after the appliqué is complete.

1. Press each background block in half vertically and horizontally. This establishes a center grid in the background that will line up with the center grid on the positioning overlay. When the backgrounds are pieced, the seamlines are the grid lines, and you do not need to press creases for centering.

Press to create a centering grid.

2. Draw a ¼"-long mark over each end of the pressed-in grid lines with a pencil. Be sure not to make the lines too long or they will show on the block. These little lines will make it easier to match up the overlay as you work with it.

3. Draw a little "X" in *one corner* of the block background with a pencil. This "X" will be in the same corner as the "X" that you draw on the overlay.

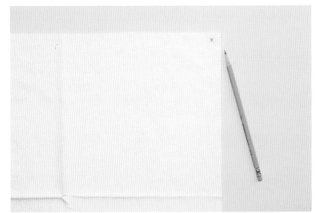

Draw ¼" long lines at each end of the pressed-in grid. Draw one small "X" in one corner.

Making the Appliqué Templates

Each appliqué shape requires a template, and we have a unique way to make templates that is both easy and accurate.

1. Use a photocopier to make 2–5 copies of each block. If the patterns need to be enlarged, make the enlargement as noted *before* making copies. Compare the copies with the original to be sure they are accurate.

2. Cut out groups of appliqué shapes from these copies. Leave a little paper allowance around each group. Where one shape overlaps another, cut the top shape from one copy and the bottom shape from another copy.

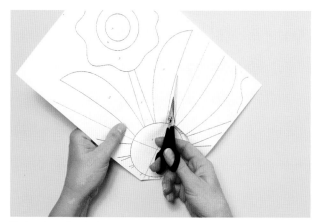

Cut out appliqué shapes.

3. Take a self-laminating sheet and place it shiny side down on the table. Peel off the paper backing, leaving the sticky side of the sheet facing up.

4. If you are doing hand appliqué, place the templates **drawn** side down on the self-laminating sheet. For fusible appliqué, place the **blank** side down. Take care when placing each template onto the laminate. Use more laminating sheets as necessary.

*Place appliqué shapes **drawn** side down on self-laminating sheets for hand appliqué.*

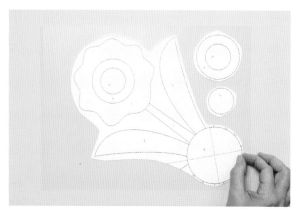

*Place appliqué shapes **blank** side down on self-laminating sheets for fusible appliqué.*

5. Cut out each individual shape. Try to split the drawn line—don't cut inside or outside of the line. Keep edges smooth and points sharp.

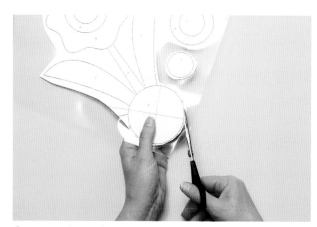

Cut out each template.

You'll notice how easy these templates are to cut out. That's the main reason we like this method. It is also true that a mechanical copy of the pattern is more accurate than hand tracing onto template plastic. As you use the templates, you will see that they are sturdy and hold up to repeated use.

Using the Templates for Hand Appliqué

For needle-turn (hand) appliqué, the templates are used right side up on the right side of the fabric.

1. Place the appliqué fabric right side up on a sandpaper board.

2. Place the template right side up (shiny laminate side up) on the fabric so that as many edges as possible are on the diagonal grain of the fabric. A bias edge is easier to turn under than one on the straight of grain.

3. Trace around the template. The sandpaper will hold the fabric in place while you trace. You will not get a sharp chalk line on flannel or wool, because these fabrics are too fuzzy, but the sandpaper board will help hold these looser weaves in place. Just be sure to draw the line right up next to the edge of the template. It won't matter that the line is wide. It gets turned under.

Place templates with as many edges as possible on the bias and trace around each template.

4. Cut out each piece, adding a ³⁄₁₆" turn-under allowance.

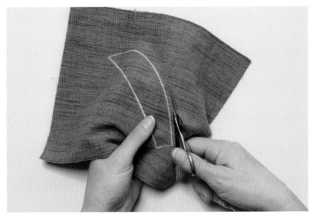

Cut out each piece, adding a ³⁄₁₆" turn-under allowance.

5. Prepare the appliqué pieces for a block, and follow the instructions on pages 65–68 to make and use the positioning overlay.

Using the Templates for Fusible Appliqué

For fusible appliqué, templates are used with the drawn side down (shiny laminate side up) on the wrong side of the fabric. Use a non-stick pressing cloth to protect the iron and ironing board. We have reservations about using fusible web with flannel, so if you do choose to use fusible web with flannel, be sure to test the fabrics you plan to use. We also recommend that you stitch around the outside of all fused appliqué pieces either by hand or machine. A blanket stitch works well.

1. Follow the manufacturer's instructions on the fusible web and iron it to the **wrong** side of the appliqué fabric. Do not peel off the paper backing.

*Iron fusible web to the **wrong** side of fabric.*

2. Leave the fabric right side down. Place the template drawn side down (shiny laminate side up) and trace around it onto the paper backing of the fusible web.

Trace around template onto paper backing.

3. Cut out the appliqué pieces on the drawn line. Add a scant ³⁄₁₆" allowance to any part of an appliqué piece that lies under another piece.

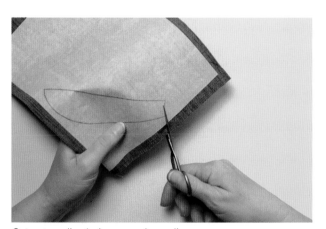

Cut out appliqué pieces on drawn line.

4. Prepare the appliqué pieces for a block, then follow the instructions below to make and use the positioning overlay.

Making the Positioning Overlay

The positioning overlay is a piece of medium-weight clear upholstery vinyl that is used to position each appliqué piece accurately on the block. The overlay is easy to make and use, and it makes your projects portable.

1. Cut a piece of the upholstery vinyl, with its tissue paper lining, to the finished size of each block. Set the tissue paper aside until you are ready to fold or store the overlay.

2. Make a copy of the patterns in this book to work from. Enlarge as directed. Tape pattern pieces together as needed.

3. Tape the copy of a pattern onto a table.

4. Tape the upholstery vinyl over the pattern. Use a ruler and a Sharpie Ultra Fine Point Marker to draw the pattern's horizontal and vertical center lines onto the vinyl.

Tape vinyl over pattern and draw center lines.

5. Trace all the lines from the pattern accurately onto the vinyl. The numbers on the pattern indicate stitching sequence—include these numbers on the overlay.

6. Draw one small "X" in one corner of the placement overlay.

Trace pattern onto the vinyl. Draw one small "X" in one corner of the overlay.

Using the Positioning Overlay for Hand Appliqué

1. Place the background right side up on the work surface. We like to work on top of our sandpaper board. The sandpaper keeps the background from shifting as you position the appliqué on the block.

2. Place the overlay right side up on top of the background.

3. Line up the center grid of the fabric or the seamlines with the center grid of the overlay. Place the "X" on the overlay in the same corner as the "X" on the block.

4. Pin the overlay if necessary to keep it from shifting out of position.

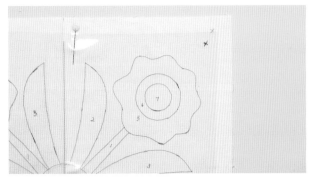

Place overlay on background and line up grids.

5. Before placing appliqué pieces on the block, finger-press the turn-under allowances. **This is a very important step.** As you finger-press, make sure that the drawn line is pressed to the back. You'll be amazed at how much easier this one step makes needle-turning the turn-under allowance.

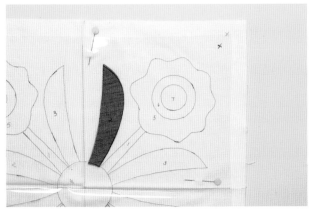

Finger-press each piece with the drawn line to the back.

6. Place the first piece under the overlay but on top of the background. It is easy to tell when the appliqué pieces are in position under the overlay. As you work, finger-press and position one piece at a time. Be sure to follow the appliqué order.

Use overlay to position appliqué pieces.

7. Fold the overlay back and pin the appliqué pieces in place using ½" sequin pins. You can pin against the sandpaper board. It does not dull the pins. We generally position and stitch only one or two pieces at a time. Remove the vinyl overlay before stitching.

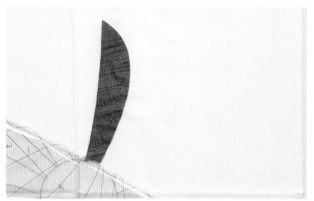

Pin appliqué piece in place.

8. Hand appliqué the pieces in place with an invisible stitch and matching thread.

9. When you are ready to put away the overlay, place the saved tissue paper over the drawn side before you fold it. The tissue paper keeps the lines from transferring from one part of the vinyl to another.

For Your Information

We don't trim the fabric behind our appliqué. We believe leaving the background intact makes the quilt stronger. And, should the quilt ever need to be repaired, it's easier if the background has not been cut.

Using the Positioning Overlay for Fusible Appliqué

1. Place the background right side up on the ironing board.

2. Place the overlay right side up on top of the background.

3. Line up the center grid of the fabric or the seamlines with the center grid of the overlay. Place the "X" on the overlay in the same corner as the "X" on the block.

Place overlay on background and line up grids.

4. Peel off the paper backing from each appliqué piece as you go. Be careful not to stretch or ravel the outer edges.

5. Place the appliqué pieces right side up, under the overlay but on top of the background. Start with the #1 appliqué piece and follow the appliqué order. It is easy to tell when the appliqué pieces are in position under the overlay. You may be able to position several pieces at once.

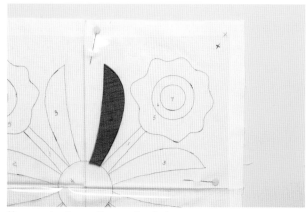

Use overlay to position appliqué pieces.

6. Carefully remove the overlay and iron the appliqué pieces in place. Be sure to follow the manufacturer's instructions for your brand of fusible web. Do not touch the overlay vinyl with the iron because the vinyl will melt.

Fuse appliqué pieces in place.

7. After fusing cotton fabric, we sew the raw edges of the fused appliqué by hand or on the sewing machine using matching thread and a straight or blanket stitch. As the quilts are used, the stitching keeps the edges secure.

Pressing and Trimming the Blocks

1. Press the blocks on the wrong side after the appliqué is complete. If the ironing surface is hard, place the blocks on a towel and the appliqué will not get flattened. Be careful not to stretch the blocks as you press.

2. Carefully trim each block to size. Measure from the center out, and always make sure the design is properly aligned with the ruler before you cut off the excess fabric.

Finishing the Quilt

1. Assemble the quilt top following the instructions for each project.

2. Construct the back of the quilt, piecing as needed.

3. Place the backing right side down on a firm surface. Tape it down to keep it from moving around while you are basting.

4. Place the batting over the backing and pat out any wrinkles.

5. Center the quilt top right side up over the batting.

6. Baste the layers together. Yes, we hand baste for both hand and machine quilting.

7. Quilt by hand or machine.

8. Trim the outer edges. Leave ¼"–⅜" of backing and batting extending beyond the edge of the quilt top. This extra fabric and batting will fill the binding nicely.

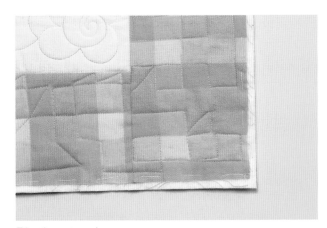

Trim the outer edges.

9. Finish the outer edges with continuous bias binding. (Refer to pages 71–72.) Sew on any hard embellishments (buttons, beads, etc.) now.

Making a Label and Sleeve

1. Make a hanging sleeve and attach it to the back of the quilt.

2. Make a label and sew it to the back of the quilt. Include information you want people to know about the quilt. Your name and address, the date, the fiber content of the quilt and batting, if it was made for a special person or occasion—these are all things that can go on the label.

Special Techniques

Cutaway Appliqué

The cutaway technique makes it much easier to stitch irregular, long, thin, or very small pieces. It is especially good to use for stems, basket handles, and stars.

1. Place the template on top of the selected fabric. Be sure to place the template on the fabric so that most of the edges will be on the diagonal grain of the fabric. Trace around the template.

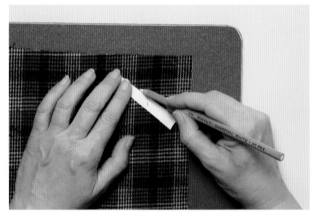

Place template with as many edges as possible on the bias and trace around the template.

2. Cut out the appliqué piece, leaving 1" or more of excess fabric around the traced shape. Leave fabric intact in the "V" between points, inside the basket handle, and so on.

3. Finger-press, making sure the drawn line is pressed to the back.

4. Use the vinyl overlay to position the appliqué piece on the block.

5. Place pins ¼" away from the edges that will be stitched first. Place pins parallel to the edges. When a shape is curved, always sew the concave side first if possible.

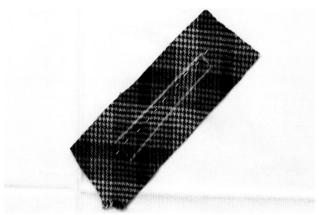

Pin appliqué piece in place.

6. Begin cutting the excess fabric away from where you will start stitching, leaving a ³⁄₁₆" turn-under allowance. Never start at an inner or outer point.

Cut away excess fabric and begin stitching.

7. Trim away more fabric as you sew. Clip inner curves and points as needed.

8. Remove the pins as you stitch the next side of the piece. Clip away excess fabric as necessary.

9. Continue until all sides of the appliqué piece are stitched.

Circle Appliqué

When sewing outer curves and circles, you can only control one stitch at a time. Use the needle or a wooden toothpick to smooth out any pleats that form. Remember, the more you practice, the better you'll get.

1. Trace circles onto the selected fabric. Cut out each circle, adding a ³⁄₁₆" turn-under allowance.

2. Finger-press the turn-under allowance, making sure the drawn line is pressed to the back.

3. Use the vinyl overlay to position the appliqué piece. Pin it in place. Use at least 2 pins to keep the circle from shifting.

4. Begin sewing. Turn under only enough turn-under allowance to take 1 or 2 stitches. If you turn under more, the appliqué will have flat spaces and points.

Turn under only enough for 1 or 2 stitches.

5. Use the tip of the needle to reach under the appliqué to spread open any folds and to smooth out any points.

6. To close the circle, turn under the last few stitches all at once. The circle will tend to flatten out.

7. Use the tip of the needle to smooth out the pleats in the turn-under allowance and to pull the flattened part of the circle into a more rounded shape.

Finish stitching circle.

Off-the-Block Construction

It is sometimes easier to sew appliqué pieces together "off the block" and then sew them as a unit to the block. Use this technique when appliqué pieces are stacked one on top of the other.

1. Choose the fabrics that make up the appliqué. Trace around the templates onto the respective fabrics. Cut out the appliqué pieces, leaving enough excess fabric around them so the pieces are easy to hold on to.

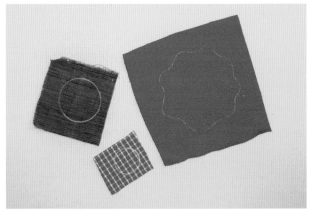

Trace and cut appliqué pieces.

2. In off-the-block construction you work from the top down. Cut out the top piece, leaving a ³⁄₁₆" turn-under allowance. Finger-press it and position it over the 2nd from the top piece. Pin the top piece in place and sew it down.

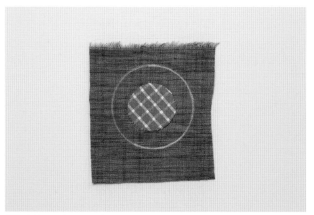

Work from the top down.

3. Trim away the excess fabric from the newly created unit, leaving a ³⁄₁₆" turn-under allowance. Finger-press it and position it over next piece down. Pin the combined unit in place and sew it down.

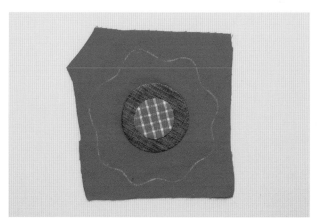

Trim excess and position over next piece.

4. Trim away the excess fabric from the unit, leaving a ³⁄₁₆" turn-under allowance. It is ready to be finger-pressed and positioned on the block.

Making Continuous Bias Binding

We find this method for making continuous bias to be particularly easy. A surprisingly small amount of fabric makes quite a bit of bias, and there is no waste. We show you how to master those tricky binding corners on pages 73–74.

We normally make our bindings 2½" wide, but we found that a 3" width was better when using flannel fabric for the binding.

1. Start with a square of fabric and cut it in half diagonally.

2. Sew the two triangles together, right sides together, as shown. Be sure to sew the edges that are on the straight of grain. If you are using striped fabric, match the stripes. You may need to offset the fabric a little to make the stripes match.

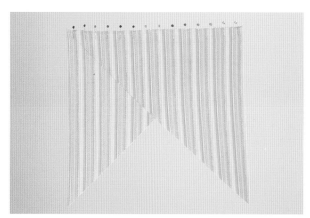

Sew straight-of-grain edges of triangles together.

3. Press the seam allowances open. Make a cut 4" deep into each side as shown.

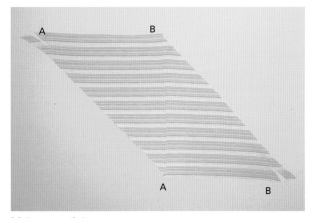

Make a cut 4" deep.

4. Match the A's and B's with the fabric right sides together. Pin and sew. Press the seam open.

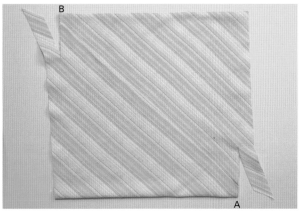

Pin and sew. Press.

5. Use a rotary cutter and ruler to cut the continuous bias strip 3" wide.

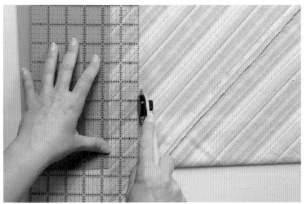

Cut to the desired width.

6. Press the continuous binding strip in half lengthwise, wrong sides together.

Cutting Tip for Continuous Bias

Try putting a small cutting mat on the end of the ironing board. Slide the tube of fabric over the mat. Use a ruler and rotary cutter to cut a long strip of continuous bias, rotating the tube of fabric as needed.

Cut using gentle pressure—if the ironing board is padded, the cutting surface may give if you press very hard.

Making Scrappy Bias Binding

Sometimes a quilt calls for a scrappy binding. Here's how to make it.

1. Cut strips 3" wide on the true bias grain of the fabric. Cut as many strips as necessary to make the length of bias required.

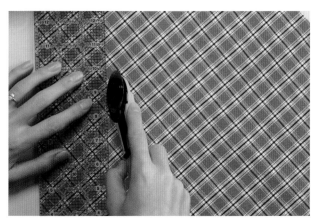

Cut 3" wide strips on the true bias of the fabric.

2. Sew the strips together end to end. Be sure to extend the points of fabric on either end of this seam ¼".

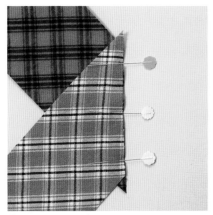

Sew the bias strips together end to end.

3. Press the continuous binding strip in half lengthwise, wrong sides together.

Sewing Binding to the Quilt

1. Cut the first end of the binding at a 45° angle. Turn this end under ½" and press.

2. Press the continuous binding strip in half lengthwise, wrong sides together.

3. With raw edges even, pin the binding to the edge of the quilt beginning a few inches away from a corner. Start sewing 6" from the beginning of the binding strip, using a ¼" seam allowance.

4. Stop ¼" away from the corner and backstitch several stitches.

Stop ¼" away from corner. Backstitch.

5. Fold the binding straight up as shown. Note the 45° angle.

Fold binding up.

6. Fold the binding straight down and begin sewing the next side of the quilt.

Fold binding down and begin sewing.

7. Sew the binding to all sides of the quilt, following the process above for the corners. Stop a few inches before you reach the beginning of the binding, but don't trim the excess binding yet.

8. Overlap the ends of the binding and cut the second end at a 90° angle. Be sure to cut the binding long enough so the cut end is covered completely by the angled end.

9. Slip the end that is cut at 90° into the angled end.

Slip 90° end into angled end.

10. Pin the joined ends to the quilt and finish sewing the binding to the quilt.

11. Turn the binding to the back of the quilt, covering the raw edges. If there is too much batting, trim enough away to leave the binding nicely filled. Hand stitch the folded edge of the binding to the back of the quilt.

Piecing Instructions

Squares and triangle-squares are wonderful. These simple shapes can be combined in so many different ways. They are perfect companions for appliqué.

Strip-Pieced Four-Patches

1. Cut strips as directed by the project instructions.

2. Sew 1 light strip to 1 dark strip. Press toward the dark fabric.

3. Cut the number of units directed by the instructions. These units will be the width of 1 strip. For example, if you cut strips 2½" wide, the units will be 2½" wide.

Cut units the width of 1 strip.

4. Sew the units together, alternating the light and dark squares, to make Four-Patches.

Sew units together to make Four-Patches.

Strip-Pieced Nine-Patches

1. Cut strips as directed by the project instructions.

2. Sew 1 dark strip to each side of 1 light strip. Press toward the dark fabric.

3. Cut the number of dark units directed by the instructions. These units will be the width of 1 strip. For example, if you cut strips 2½" wide, the units will be 2½" wide.

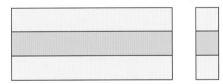

Cut dark units the width of 1 strip.

4. Sew 1 light strip to each side of 1 dark strip. Press toward the dark fabric.

5. Cut the number of light units directed by the instructions.

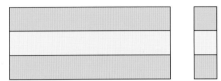

Cut light units the width of 1 strip.

6. Sew light and dark units together to make light or dark Nine-Patches as directed by the instructions.

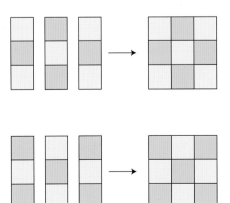

Make light or dark Nine-Patches.

Triangle-Squares

1. Cut squares as directed by the project instructions.

2. Place a light square over a dark square, right sides together.

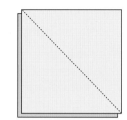

Place squares right sides together.

3. Sew them together on the diagonal. If the flannel is slipping, pin the squares together.

4. Cut away the excess fabric, leaving a ¼" seam allowance.

Cut away excess fabric, leaving a ¼" seam allowance.

5. Press toward the dark fabric.

No-Mark Diagonals

Place a ruler squarely on the bed of the machine. Line up one side of the ruler with the spot where the needle goes through the throat plate. Stick a 3"– 4" piece of painter's tape on the table (not the throat plate) next to the ruler.

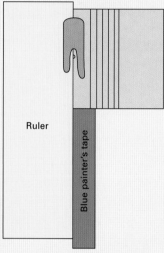

Place the ruler squarely on the bed of the machine. Stick 3"–4" of painter's tape to the table next to the ruler.

As you sew, the far point of the 2 squares will follow the left edge of the painter's tape, giving you a straight seam.

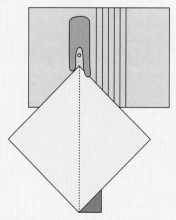

The far end of the squares follows the edge of the tape.

About the Authors

The Green Country Quilter's Guild in Tulsa, Oklahoma, can be credited for bringing Linda Jenkins and Becky Goldsmith together. Their friendship developed while they worked together on many guild projects and through a shared love for appliqué. This partnership led to the birth of Piece O' Cake Designs in 1994 and survived Linda's move to Pagosa Springs, Colorado, and then back to Tulsa in 2001, while Becky headed for Sherman, Texas.

Linda owned and managed a beauty salon before she started quilting. Over the years she developed a fine eye for color as a hair colorist and makeup artist. Becky's degree in interior design and many art classes provided a perfect background for quilting. Linda and Becky have shown many quilts and won numerous awards. Together they make a dynamic quilting duo and love to teach other quilters the joys of appliqué.

In the fall of 2002 Becky and Linda joined the C&T Publishing family, where they continue to produce wonderful books and patterns.

Look for more Piece O' Cake books from C&T Publishing

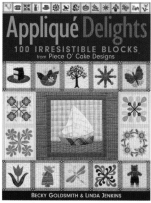

Appliqué Delights

Flowering Favorites

A Slice of Christmas

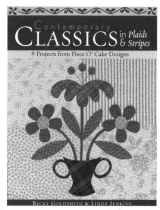

Contemporary Classics in Plaids & Stripes

The Appliqué Sampler

For information about individual Piece O' Cake patterns, contact C&T Publishing.

Index

Projects

Useful Information

Resources

For More Information

Ask for a free catalog:
C&T Publishing, Inc.
P.O. Box 1456
Lafayette, CA 94549
800-284-1114
email: ctinfo@ctpub.com
website: www.ctpub.com

Resources

Piece O' Cake Designs
website: www.pieceocake.com

Quilting Supplies
Cotton Patch Mail Order
3404 Hall Lane
Dept CTB
Lafayette, CA 94549
800-835-4418   925-283-7883
email: quiltusa@yahoo.com
website: www.quiltusa.com

Note: Fabrics used in the quilts shown may not be currently available because fabric manufacturers keep most fabrics in print for only a short time.

Booklist

For more information, ask for a free catalog:

C&T Publishing, Inc.
P.O. Box 1456
Lafayette, CA 94549
(800) 284-1114
Email: ctinfo@ctpub.com
Website: www.ctpub.com